The Waiting Room

FELICIA M. WRIGHT

PAGE PUBLISHING, INC.
Conneaut Lake, PA

First originally published by Page Publishing 2021

Unless otherwise indicated, all Scripture quotations
are taken from the *King James Version* of the Bible.

ISBN 978-1-6624-3105-0 (pbk)
ISBN 978-1-6624-5275-8 (hc)
ISBN 978-1-6624-3106-7 (digital)

Printed in the United States of America

To all *Waiting Room* Warriors—
past, present, and future

In loving memory of Margie Wright,
my beautiful mother-in-law
and Patricia Teats, my tenacious but elegant mentor

Although you are no longer physically here, you are still loved. Your legacy of love, hope, and commitment to others will continue to live on in my heart and in the hearts of my husband and children.

Contents

Acknowledgments

With a heart of gratitude,

To my husband, Martin, thank you for your love, prayers, and being extremely supportive of me in all of my ventures throughout the years, especially this writing project.

To my children Jessica, Ashley, and Brandon thank you for your love, support, prayers, and causing it to never be a dull moment in our home. Jessica and Ashley, the two of you are the most adorable cheerleaders and accountability partners ever!

To my parents, Lawrence Williams and Joy Thomas, thank you for your love, support, prayers, and guidance. Also for raising me to be a courageous, creative, and independent individual.

To my Auntie Joyce, thank you for your love, support, prayers, and willingness to let me share a glimpse of our very special sisters-in-the-Lord friendship.

To my Uncle Andrew, thank you for your love, prayers, and for being a supportive accountability partner. Your persistent but gentle encouragement is what I needed to finish this writing project.

To Don Staley, thank you for your support and encouragement. Your passion for writing has truly been an inspiration to me.

To the rest of my village of accountability partners, my siblings, sisters-in-law, my extended family members, college friends, church family, employer and coworkers thank you all for your love, support, and prayers.

Most of all, I would like to say thank you to my Heavenly Father, His Son Jesus Christ, and the Holy Spirit for abundantly loving me and for giving me the conceptual creativity to write and bring this book into existence.

Introduction

When you know deep in your heart beyond a shadow of a doubt that your loved one has been predestined for greatness, you are in a constant state of anticipation as you wait for that greatness to come to fruition. That greatness is God's plan for their lives manifested in its fullness. With the discovery and acceptance of the future that God wants for them, His vision for their lives becomes their own vision as well. Then God and your loved one become unified in purpose and vision.

God's first plan for our loved ones is for them to accept His Son, Jesus Christ, as their Lord and Savior. Then connect with a church that will teach and grow them spiritually to develop them into mature Christians. As they allow Jesus to be Lord over their lives, God's vision for them will obtain momentum and vitality.

Waiting for the fruition of that vision to become manifested causes you to stay in a state of expectancy. You must stay focused and remain consistent in prayer as you wait for the physical manifestation of God's will and purpose to come to past in their lives.

This is a waiting process that transports you into their spiritual "waiting room." Your assignment to this destination can become infinite. The acceptance of your assignment will require faith, a high level of patience, along with complete trust and dependency on God.

We must develop and maintain a consistent prayer life. I would suggest that you get involved with a prayer group or get a prayer partner. These individuals should be trustworthy and people of high integrity because you will need to be transparent and vulnerable with them. Follow the leading of the Holy Spirit as to who you should develop these types of friendships with. From my own personal experience, I have found that it was the sisterhood relationships of Christian women that helped me during the *waiting room* periods in my own life. I am grateful for the supportiveness of my sisters-in-the Lord relationships with my mother, aunts, daughters, and sisters. I am also appreciative of the friendships with women that I believe God Himself put into my life. These are friendships that developed because we were colleagues, church members, and even neighbors. Each one of these sisterhood relationships developed at their own designated time and season in my life. These women have that "we got you" mentality. They cover me with their love and prayers. I have developed a strong sense of what true Christian sisterhood is because of these women.

If you are a male, I strongly suggest that your prayer partner and/or prayer group regarding this should be primarily men. Men are just more comfortable talking with other men after they have finally let their guard down. To put it mildly, there are less distractions, and men need to be accountable to other men. Ask God to send you a prayer partner and or group. They will be the people that you can be real with and have the freedom to share what's on your heart. These individuals will become your spiritual siblings and may even become mentors to you. They will also help protect your heart by building you up and keeping you covered in prayer.

Waiting patiently for our family members to begin to walk in the vision God has for their lives will also require us to be steadfast and unmovable. We must remain strong and trust God, understanding that it is His will and desire to bring His vision to past in their lives. I believe every Christian has the capacity to dig deep within themselves with the assistance of the Holy Spirit to help birth this greatness through spending time with God in prayer, fasting, praise, and worship.

Regardless if your loved one is a spouse, child, parent, extended family member, neighbor, friend, or someone in the workplace, God wants to use you as a person of influence along with you continually praying for them. It doesn't matter the nature of the relationship or the role you have in their life; your influence is vital and instrumental to you being in their spiritual *Waiting Room.*

Chapter 1

―――――◆◆◆―――――

The Waiting Room

A waiting room can be both physical and spiritual. The physical waiting room is a holding terminal for those of us who are awaiting answers to questions or the presentation of something great. Any building with a room can be used as a waiting room. Most of us are familiar with a lobby, office, and a hospital waiting room. Normally, the atmosphere here is not a place of rest but a place of great expectation, anxiety, and uncertainty.

I would like to talk to you about the spiritual waiting room. This room doesn't have physical walls. It is the intangible space that we carry people in our hearts. When we take on the act of caring for the well-being of someone, those emotions connect us to them spiritually. The place that we wait in as our loved ones begin to align their will with the will of God is what I like to call the spiritual *waiting room*. As we wait in expectation, our waiting must not be in vain. During this time period, we must pray that they will start to understand, position, and accept God's plan for their lives.

For some people, this process may take just a few months; but for others, it could take several years to start and complete the process. The same emotions that we may experience in a physical, tangible waiting room will also be present in our spiritual *waiting room*. If your loved one is in the several years process time period, you will be tempted to give in to your emotions and lose hope. But God is faithful; He has already given you the tools that you will need to help you stay in faith and overcome any feelings of doubt.

There are certain roles that we have and tools that we must utilize while we are in their waiting room. The primary tool we have available to us is God's written Word, which is known as the Bible. May I suggest that you get an additional version of the Bible like an Amplified Version to better assist you in your understanding and clarifying the scriptures that are in the King James Version (KJV). You don't have to be a Bible scholar to use these tools. They are very useful tools for us when we not only read, study, and meditate but implement them in our daily lives. When this is done, we will gain understanding, wisdom, patience, and revelation during our time spent in our loved one's waiting room.

Whether it is during your own personal study time, a Bible group study, or studying the Bible during a church service, it is imperative that we read our Bibles daily. Meditating on the scriptures in the

Bible will give you encouragement when you become weary of standing in faith for your loved one. Ask God for help; He will strengthen and sustain you, just as it is written in Isaiah 40:29–31,

> He giveth power to the faint; and to them that have no might he increaseth strength. Even the youths shall faint and be weary, and the young men shall utterly fall: But they that wait upon the LORD shall renew their strength; they shall mount up with wings as eagles; they shall run, and not be weary; and they shall walk, and not faint.

Let's take a look at the roles of an *intercessor* and an *exhorter*. I believe these are the two major roles that we carry out while we are in our loved one's waiting room. An intercessor is someone who intercedes on the behalf of another individual through prayer. To put it another way, an intercessor is the go-between person. Those of us who have siblings understand the importance of a go-between person. This was the sibling we would strongly encourage to ask our parents for something that our parents may have told us no to, but instead we sent the go-between sibling hoping to get a more favorable response. In many situations the go-between sibling was the youngest.

They weren't old enough to understand that they were being set up.

However, being the go-between person when it comes to interceding for our loved ones is far more powerful than the example I just mentioned. This is a powerful role because it allows you to activate your faith for your loved one on their behalf. God accepts your prayers for them. When He hears your voice praying for them, He hears with open and receptive ears because we are now representing them. You are pleading their case for them just like a lawyer in the courtroom. God recognizes you as their intercessor and accepts your prayers for them in the same manner He would if they were praying for themselves. As you earnestly intercede for your loved one, you implement Ephesians 6:18, "Praying always with all prayer and supplication in the Spirit, and watching thereunto with all perseverance and supplication for all saints."

The Holy Spirit also operates as an intercessor. Let's take a look at the scriptures in Romans 8:26–27,

> Likewise the Spirit also helpeth our infirmities: for we know not what we should pray for as we ought: but the Spirit itself maketh intercession for us with groanings which cannot be uttered. And he that searcheth the hearts knoweth what is the mind of the Spirit, because he

maketh intercession for the saints
according to the will of God.

You have just partnered up with the *Greatest Intercessor*. Wow! Now that is an awesome partnership. The Holy Spirit has your back, and as you pray for your loved one, the Holy Spirit joins in with you to assist, encourage, and comfort you. You don't have to feel like you are in this by yourself; you are in good company. There may be times when you feel like giving up and your prayers aren't working; that's when the Holy Spirit will comfort and strengthen you to persevere.

As you intercede for your loved one, allow the Holy Spirit to guide you as to how to specifically pray for them. You may be led to pray a particular bible verse over them, sing songs of praise and worship, to fast, or to just sit quietly in God's presence. The key here is to follow the leading of the Holy Spirit. We don't want our prayers to become ritualistic or mundane. We want our prayers for our loved ones to remain effective, full of power, and fervency. This will be accomplished when we stay connected to and follow the leading of the Holy Spirit.

For example, the scripture that I prayed over my husband the most when he was having challenges in the workplace was Isaiah 54:17, "No weapon that is formed against thee shall prosper; and every tongue that shall rise against thee in judgment thou shalt condemn. This is the heritage of the servants of the LORD, and their righteousness is of me, saith the

LORD." I would simply say, "Lord, Your Word says that no weapon that is formed against Martin shall prosper, and every tongue that rises up against him in judgment Martin shall condemn." By doing this, I was saying what my Heavenly Father said about the situation. This allowed the power of God to show up every time. Sometimes it took a while for things to change for the better, but they eventually changed. When we profess God's written Word over unfavorable circumstances, we are professing the solution, not rehearsing the problem. This also puts us in agreement with God according to the scripture in Matthew 24:35, "Heaven and earth shall pass away, but my words shall not pass away." God's Word is not void of power.

Singing songs of praise and worship also releases the power of God. I remember a particular time during my college years, my friends and I were completely stressed out. It was the end of the semester, and we were studying for our final exams. Someone suggested that we have a praise-and-worship session. We did just that; we praised and worshipped God as if we were at a concert. We were the musicians and the band. God was in the audience receiving our praises and honored by our worship. We created an environment for God to inhabit according to Psalm 22:3, "But thou art holy, O thou that inhabitest the praises of Israel." Another way of saying this is, God dwells in our praises of Him. Our stress and anxiety subsided. We had peace and confidence going into our finals. That was so long ago I don't remember everyone's individual outcome on their exams, but we took the focus off the challenge before us and praised God for the victory. We did obtain the victory. Everyone eventually graduated and went on to pursue their chosen careers.

Now let's talk about fasting. Fasting is the act of abstaining from something. As we put the act of fasting into practice, our focus should be on sacrificing more of our time—quality time, that is—with God in prayer. Spending more quality time with God is the objective so that we can hear Him more clearly. It is during this time that we can receive clarity, additional instructions, or even correction.

When it comes to fasting, let's understand that it is not always about fasting from food. Some people may not have a problem with giving up food (they don't require much food because they have small appetites) while some of us have heartier appetites. We are always trying a new recipe, planning our next meal, and trying to fit a trip to our local bulk warehouse store into our already busy day so that we can sample the samples. During the times when my daughters and I would fast together corporately, I encouraged them to give up something that they thought they couldn't live without.

My youngest daughter Ashley, when she was eighteen years old, was very petite, lean, and at times an annoying picky eater. My husband and I would have to remind her to eat, so having her fast from food was not a good idea. Naturally speaking, it would not have been a sacrifice for her spiritually. I had to keep in mind that what she deemed important to her existence as a teenager varied from week to week, but it usually had something to do with her social life, fashion, and technology. Therefore, I encouraged her to pick something that she believed she would be able to comply with.

Once my teenagers obtained the concept of fasting and were willing to incorporate it into their lives, I wanted them to be reasonable with the choice of what they were fasting from. For example, my husband and I have used taking their cell phones from them as a form of discipline. On one occasion when it was time to fast, Ashley picked fasting from using her cell phone. Meanwhile, Ashley had gotten her cell phone taken from her some time prior to the fast. She had adjusted to not having her cell phone so well I had forgotten momentarily that we had taken it from her. When I remembered that she didn't have her cell phone, I said to her, "Ashley, you are not being reasonable. You don't have your cell phone! How are you going to fast from something you don't even have?" She snickered at me. Ashley and I are the practical jokesters in my family; no doubt Little Miss Ashley enjoyed her short-lived moment of outwitting me.

She eventually picked something to fast from, and it was candy. At that time, Ashley loved candy, especially the sour chewy kind. She didn't buy any candy during this time period of fasting, and whenever she wanted to eat some candy, she prayed. In the end, Ashley finished her fasting strong. She experienced a sense of accomplishment. She started a fast that she was able to finish. She wasn't eating candy on a daily basis. Therefore, she got a little healthier; but most importantly, she obtained more insight from God on what she had been praying for.

I would now like to discuss with you your role as an *exhorter*. Another way to describe this role is to call you an encourager or a cheerleader. We all have experienced firsthand what a cheerleader does. Either we have been cheerleaders at school or know someone who was or is a cheerleader. In the world of sports, the cheerleaders are there to support their team players and to cheer them on to victory. When players don't have someone cheering and rooting for them as they face a possible defeat, they have a hard time keeping their heads in the game. This can explain why having the home-field advantage is favored among teams. The team that is playing at home can depend on their fans, family members, and their team's cheerleaders to cheer them on throughout the game. They can pull from the excitement and positive energy, which may possibly cause them to win the game.

Cheerleaders help keep the players encouraged throughout the game and continually remind them of their purpose for being there, which is to win. That's our purpose also to help our loved ones win in the game of life. God is counting on us to be their personal cheerleader. Although our purpose here is more spiritual than natural, we must help them remain spiritually confident by encouraging them when needed and continually reminding them who they are in God.

Some people are just naturally encouragers; it's one of the personality traits God designed them with. At some point in our lives, we have been around an encouraging person; and after being around them for a period of time, that personality trait affected us in a very positive way. Being around them helped stir up things in our own spirit and helped transform us into becoming an *exhorter*—which is all a part of God's master plan. He had someone be an exhorter to us for our own personal benefit with the objective that someday we would, in return, become an exhorter to someone else.

One of my closest friends is an exhorter. Before I got to know her on a personal level, I remember seeing her at church encouraging people, smiling, laughing, and greeting people with hugs. My thoughts were, *There is something genuinely different about her.* When we were finally formally introduced, she greeted me with a smile, a hug, and a compliment. The hug was full of Christian love. What I mean is she hugged me as if she had known me my entire life. This is how she was with everyone. She has a laugh that is truly contagious. She also has a cheerful heart and is pleasant to be around. The Bible says in the first part of Proverbs 15:13, "A merry heart maketh a cheerful countenance"—and this is true of my friend. Her attribute of being an exhorter made it very easy for me to receive this role that God had planned for her to have in my life. She has also become my "spiritual big sister."

As God uses me as an exhorter in the lives of others, I have a clearer understanding of the role my friend has played in my life, and I am sincerely grateful for her and her friendship. The following chapters will help you identify whose *waiting room* you are in. You will gain a clearer understanding of why God has placed you there in the first place. Lastly, you will become better equipped to carry out your purpose while assisting your loved one in becoming all that God has created them to be.

Chapter 2

Your Spouse

I have experienced firsthand the extreme importance of effectively utilizing my prayer time while in my husband Martin's *waiting room.* God's protection and safety is something that I consistently pray for regarding my husband. My most crucial prayer for safety and protection is to plead *the blood* of Jesus over my husband, along with several scriptures. One of my go-to scriptures for protection and safety is Proverbs 30:5, "Every word of God is pure: he is a shield unto them that put their trust in him." I understand that God's Word is pure. Fully comprehending the usage of a shield made me aware of the importance of this scripture as I declare it over my husband. You see, a shield covers you. It defends you with the intentional purpose of protecting you from hurt, harm, and dangers that are seen and unseen.

Martin, along with everyone else, needs God to be their shield on a daily basis, especially while cruising around in a motorized vehicle. It does not matter whether you're the driver or passenger; you are in need of some divine heavenly protection. My husband has a long commute to and from work, so his safety has always been a concern of mine. After our children received their driver's permit, Martin assigned himself to be their "primary at-home driving instructor." He won that title hands down; I had already read the fine print. I was notably unprepared for the mental anguish that came along with his new position. Understanding that Martin had his work cut out for him, I was praying for God's protection and safety for all of them as well as a higher level of patience for my husband.

On this one particular autumn day, the air was crisp. Fall-colored leaves were aimlessly blowing in the wind. With his travel mug filled with coffee, Martin and our daughter Ashley were headed out to run some errands. Martin secretly enjoyed having our inexperienced drivers chauffeur him around town. However, that day was different. He was led to not have Ashley drive but to put on the chauffeur's hat himself. As they drove to their first destination, they were approaching a winding road.

Martin said he heard the words, *Slow down!* But they did not come from Ashley; she hadn't muttered a word and was unaware of what her daddy was experiencing. Martin also saw blue-colored streaks of an object that was indiscernible. But what he did discern was that it was God communicating with him. He listened, obeyed, and immediately, he slowed down the speed of the car. On the other side of that winding road was another car driving on the wrong side of the street cruising at a remarkable rate of speed aligned to hit my husband's car head-on. By Martin slowing down the speed of his car, he was able to respond quickly and maneuver his car to avoid what could have been an imminently dangerous car accident. After collecting himself and making sure that Ashley was okay, he realized the color of the car that he had come so close to colliding with was blue. He then surmised that this blue car was definitely the object that displayed the blue-colored streaks that were originally indiscernible in the vision that he had seen moments before the incident.

Travelers are familiar with the term "frequent flyer miles." If we could accumulate frequent flyer miles for the countless prayers and hours devoted to our time spent in the *waiting room* of a spouse we would have some serious jet lag. With the exception of our children, I am convinced the other people that we tend to pray for the most are our spouses. And we should; it is a necessity for the success and longevity of a marriage. In the marriage relationship, everything that effects your spouse will have an impact on your life as well. The two of you are joined together, doing life together up close and personal.

Above any other relationship that will have the most profound impact on our lives is the relationship that we have with our spouse. We need this relationship to remain healthy, vibrant, and peaceful. The foundation of our spousal relationship must stay void of cracks and erosion. Here are some excellent scriptures for you to incorporate as building blocks for the foundation of your relationship with your spouse:

> Put on therefore, as the elect of God, holy and beloved, bowels of mercies, kindness, humbleness of mind, meekness, longsuffering; Forbearing one another, and forgiving one another, if any man have a quarrel against any: even as Christ forgave you, so also do ye. And above all these things put on charity, which is the bond of perfectness. And let the peace of God rule in your hearts, to the which also ye are called in one body; and be ye thankful. (Colossians 3:12–15)

As we maintain the structural integrity in the foundation of our martial partnership, we should pray for them through the eyes of faith—simply put, seeing them as God sees them. God sees them having accepted Jesus Christ as their Lord and Savior. He sees them healed in their bodies and minds. He sees them victorious in every area of their lives, which also includes having a beautiful harmonious marriage with us. When we don't know better, we can exercise the tendency of having a "griping and complaining" session while we are supposed to be praying for our spouse. These sessions may allow us to feel good and vindicated since we got everything off our chest, but those feelings of euphoria will soon dissipate. What I have learned is that they are a complete waste of time and energy.

God can't intervene on our behalf when we conduct our prayer time in that manner. It's not faith-based. The Bible teaches us in Hebrews 11:6, "But without faith it is impossible to please him." There is absolutely no faith in griping and complaining, so there will be no pleasing God. When we begin to diligently and effectively pray for our spouse using faith, God is pleased. Then we are in position to receive the rest of that verse in Hebrews 11:6, which says, "for he that cometh to God must believe that he is, and that he is a rewarder of them that diligently seek him."

I don't know about you, but I like to be rewarded, especially from God. Time spent praying and interceding in faith on behalf of our spouse is a tremendous investment which will reap generous dividends when it pleases God. It will yield a double-fold blessing. We receive a reward from God, and we get to reap the benefits of our spouse getting their prayers answered. So how I see it, that's "cha-ching" big time. I noticed a preeminent change in my life when I learned to pray for my husband through the eyes of faith. While we are in our spouse's *waiting room*, let's strive to be more persistent, effective, and fervent as we pray for them through the eyes of faith.

Chapter 3

Your Children

When we become parents, our initial thoughts are how special and precious that baby is to our family. We want them to evolve, develop their own relationship with God, and fulfill the purpose He planned for their lives. God knew our children before we birthed them. According to the first part of scripture in Isaiah 44:2, "Thus saith the LORD that made thee, and formed thee from the womb, which will help thee." God formed us while we were in the womb. Another word for *form* is *create*. God is the Ultimate Creator. The Creator has a designated assignment for His creation. In other words, God has an assignment for us as well as our children. That assignment is His plan and purpose for their lives. As parents, it is our responsibility to pray for wisdom on rearing our children. And for insight regarding God's plan and purpose for their lives. Once they obtain understanding and direction on their assignment, we must do everything that we can to help them stay aligned with God's plan and purpose for their lives.

The scripture says in Psalm 127:3, "Lo, children are an heritage of the LORD: and the fruit of the womb is his reward." I want to draw your attention to the word *heritage*. Another way of viewing this word is to say that children are an inheritance—an inheritance from God. An inheritance is generally something that is of importance and deem valuable to the previous owner. It is passed down to you with the expectation that you will recognize its importance and affectionately provide the same level of devotion.

For those of us who have given birth to a baby, we can still remember certain aspects of our pregnancy. I don't think many of us fully comprehended in totality the immense responsibility that was bestowed upon us. We have been entrusted by God to guide, protect, love, and nurture our little ones. As parents, we must apply those same nurturing principles of protection, love, and guidance—but at a much higher level of intensity while we are in their spiritual waiting room.

As a parent, I personally believe the group of individuals that we tend to pray and intercede for through the duration of their lifetime are our children. The enormous responsibility of cultivating the spiritual growth and development of my children began before they were a twinkle in my eye. I prayed for each of my children prior to the conception phase and also during each of my pregnancies. But in the instance of my son, I think that I had a little more unsolicited help. My husband and I were privately discussing the possibility of having another baby, a baby boy to be exact. The thoughts of having a baby boy became prayers for a healthy baby boy.

I can remember this one occasion so vividly. My little girls came to me and asked, "Mom, why don't we have a brother?"—almost in the same inquisitive manner that all the other "Mom, why?" questions were asked. Seeing where this was headed, I was not up for a series of why questions, so I quickly jarred back at the two of them "because you both are girls," thinking that would be the end of this little discussion. I was not prepared for their response. They replied, "We are going to pray and ask God for a brother." After listening to the sincerity in their little voices, I decided to tell them that their daddy and I were already praying for them to have a baby brother.

Well, they eventually did get a baby brother. They really did believe that their prayers had something to do with their baby brother being born, and so did I. My husband was ecstatic that we had a boy. He was outnumbered coming up as a child with three older sisters and no brothers. Surely, that couldn't be his future. Outnumbered once again, married with two daughters and no other source of testosterone to assist him in the day-to-day struggle of being surrounded by girls.

When I became a parent, a constant concern for me was the well-being and safety of my children. The younger your child is, the more you can control the many variables in their environment. You can child-proof your home with all kinds of gadgets to protect and ensure the safety of your little offspring. Organized play dates turns into chaperoned school field trips and dances. During their teenage years, I had to become an orchestrator and devise strategic methods to remain several steps ahead of them.

Our children, regardless of their age and the milestone events that are happening, will always require prayers of protection from us. I pray for their protection and that God will deliver my children from all hurt, harm, and danger. Even to this day, when praying for their safety, I still profess these scriptures in Psalm 91:11–12, "For he shall give his angels charge over thee, to keep thee in all thy ways. They shall bear thee up in their hands, lest thou dash thy foot against a stone." When my son Brandon was a youngster, I would jokingly say, "The angels that are assigned to Brandon put in some serious overtime hours protecting him. That boy is always into something!" He was inquisitive, full of energy and constantly investigating the contents of my cabinets. Not to mention he stayed in perpetual movement: running, jumping, climbing, and leaping over things.

I can recall an incident that occurred when he was in the third grade. It was the end of the school day. Parents were picking their children up from their designated areas. I pulled into the parking lot and parked my car. I observed a gathering of students, teachers, and the vice principal just outside the front door of the school. I got out of my car, began to walk toward the school's front door, and noticed that someone was on the ground lying on their backside. As I proceeded closer, I could see the child's shoes protruding pass the leg of a bystander. I thought to myself, *Those shoes look very familiar.* I finally realized, to my surprise and dismay, that those shoes were—"oh my goodness, Brandon's shoes!" That was my little boy, my Brandon, lying there on his backside unresponsive. Brandon ran headfirst into the metal partition that was between the two entry doors of the school building.

The teachers and vice principal were trying to wake him up, but he wasn't responding. I kneeled down beside him and spoke into his ear, "Brandon, it's me, your mom. Wake up!" Within minutes, he was awake and alert. His sisters and I helped him to my car. After we got him into the car, he began to describe how pretty all the lights were. We didn't see any pretty lights because there weren't any, only stoplights. I said to my daughters, "Lay hands on him and pray!" I prayed in the Spirit as I drove us to the hospital.

Midway through the doctor's examination, Brandon had fully recovered. His thoughts were cohesive; he wasn't talking about any lights being pretty, and most importantly, he knew that his birthday was in a few days. He was excited about his birthday. I had planned an action-packed weekend filled with festivities and major fun.

I believe my prayers for God's protection and my daughters praying for their brother right at that moment produced our favorable outcome. Brandon was delivered from the harm of running headfirst into a metal partition. He didn't experience swelling or display symptoms of a concussion. He only had a very small scratch located in the middle of his forehead.

The next day after taking him to school, I returned to the scene of the incident. There was a large dent in the metal partition where Brandon had hit his head. Upon further inspection, there was a tiny piece of Brandon's skin still embedded in the metal partition. That explained the small scratch that he received in the middle of his forehead. Throughout the years, I have continued to pray for his protection. All three of my children have been protected from and during car accidents. They have not sustained any major injuries from the car accidents that they were involved in, and to "God be the glory!"

My children's teenage years had some turbulent moments, but remarkably, they are some of my fondest memories of them growing up. I am not the only parent who believes it was because of prayer we were able to get through our children's teenage years with not as many head-on collisions that could have transpired. As parents, we already know and comprehend the teenage years can be so volatile that you "gotta stay prayed up." As a result of having three children who were all entering into adolescence almost simultaneously, their world was always about "to end" at any moment, at least in their minds. And in my mind, I was always waiting for the other shoe to drop.

As my teenage daughters evolved into young adults, they grew to understand that a lifestyle of prayer is exactly that—a lifestyle. I recently asked my now young adult children if they could remember a specific time during their teenage years when my prayers really helped them. My daughters were very forthcoming and gave me consent to share the following occurrences. My oldest daughter Jessica, recalls our somewhat fractured relationship during some of her adolescence years; which was from the age of fourteen until right around her sweet sixteenth birthday celebration.

All of my children were late bloomers. Jessica began to bloom around the age of fourteen. She bloomed in hormones and attitude to boot. And somehow she developed this ideology that I had become her worst enemy. My once compliant, helpful, and fun-to-be-around child was now moody, argumentative, and trying to start a revolution in my home. Tired of the emotional collisions that we were experiencing, I turned to God for help. It was my earnest desire to have a good relationship with her. I began to pray according to the scripture in Psalm 37:4, "Delight thyself also in the LORD; and he shall give thee the desires of thine heart." I asked God to show me how to be a better mother to Jessica and asked Him for the keys to her heart.

Gradually, things began to change and for the better. It was during the planning of her sweet sixteenth birthday celebration that she saw me in a different light. I made this event as extravagant as I possibly could. It was all about her. She felt special, accepted, valued, and loved. She no longer viewed me as the person whose primary objective in life was to make her life miserable. I got my daughter back, but she was different. She was no longer my little girl. She had blossomed into a mature, talented, beautiful young lady with exceptional leadership capabilities and compassion for others. With God's help, we had found our way back into each other's heart.

My youngest daughter Ashley said, it was during her latter years of high school when she was dealing with depression that my prayers were very helpful to her. Along with incorporating some family intervention meetings, I continuously professed over her according to the scripture in Isaiah 54:13, "And all thy children shall be taught of the LORD; and great shall be the peace of thy children." I would say, "Great is the peace of my Ashley because she has been taught of the Lord." I prayed this over her with faith and confidence because I knew she had been taught of the Lord. My husband and I made sure that all of our children were reared in and attended children's church ministry and youth ministry. We regularly attended church and participated in church activities as a family. That scripture continues to be part of my prayers. I still profess that scripture over my children whenever I pray for them. I am grateful to have observed Ashley press forward to emerge into a lovely and confident young lady with a funny sense of humor. She has become optimistic, attentive, and on most days, she is a ray of sunshine.

A year or so ago, God gave me a new revelation regarding this scripture. He revealed to me, "Felicia's peace is great also because Felicia has been taught of Me." I am His child, and I have been taught of Him, so I began to declare and decree that Felicia's peace shall be great. When I uttered those words, there was a calmness that came to me almost immediately.

As a parent of Christian teenagers, I was fully aware of the peer pressure that my tweens faced to conform and fit in. To combat that pressure, I also prayed that they would not be ashamed of being a Christian and that they would let their "light shine" regardless of their surroundings. I had to operate in faith and confidence in order for this prayer to be effective. Well, this prayer was answered while my daughters where in high school. Since my daughters and their childhood friend arrived to school earlier than their classes began, they thought that it would be a good idea to use that time to pray. It initially started off with just the three of them. Then other students asked to pray with them, which lead to the formation of their early-morning prayer group with students from different ethnicities, cultures, and religions. They welcomed and prayed with anyone who wanted to participate. As my oldest daughter Jessica recalls, she really looked forward to their early-morning prayer sessions. It helped them through some very tough times. Especially the time when one of their classmates died in a fatal car accident. Because of the internet and social media, the grievous news traveled around the school's campus within just a few hours.

The next morning when my daughters arrived at school they were shocked to see so many students waiting on them for early-morning prayer. To see so many of their peers outside of a church event wanting and asking for prayer was overwhelming. But they understood that God wanted them to help and pray for their classmates. They prayed for the family members who had just lost their loved one and for their school. My girls and their childhood friend were acknowledged by their principal. She thanked them on behalf of their fellow classmates for their acts of compassion.

As my children became young adults, I began to adopt the notion of praying for them unselfishly. What I mean by unselfishly is that I started praying that my children become the best individuals that God wants them to become instead of who I want them to become. Praying for them not only as their mother but also as their sister-in-the Lord. This way of praying was a real game changer for me. That adjustment has allowed me to respond calmly and remain consistent in my prayers during every season of life that I am in their spiritual waiting room. This also allows me to trust God completely, knowing that with Him I am fierce enough to face any circumstance. As long as I stay focused, keep my eyes on Him and not the circumstances, He will see to it that my prayers get answered and maintain peace in my home. What I have experienced many times is that my perspective regarding the circumstances changed. There is always a brighter side to everything if we would simply adjust our vision and attitude.

Throughout Brandon's years as a high school student, he worked part-time hours, maintained good grades, and participated in martial arts. While excelling in all three, he obtained his black belt ranking in martial arts. After graduating from high school, Brandon's busy schedule made it a challenge for us to spend quality time together.

Brandon is currently working in retail, food delivery service, and he has a budding social life. His demanding schedule has everyone in our home pulling on him for their own share of quality time. A few months back when I was praying for Brandon, God gave me the idea of another way to stay connected with Brandon. It's really quite simple. I am to write Brandon monthly letters, keep them short and to the point. With emphasis on how much he is loved, appreciated, and very important to our family. The smile, the "Thanks, Ma," and the hugs that I receive from him after he reads his letters are priceless. I must say it is nice to get that response from him. But even if I didn't get anything in return from him, I would still do it—because I am sowing seeds of love into the good ground of my son's heart while I am in his *waiting room.*

Chapter 4

———◆———〰———◆———

Extended Family

The spiritual well-being of my extended family members is very important to me. It is my duty to pray and intercede for my extended family members. I believe God has strategically placed us in our families to love, support one another, and to also be a witness for Him to our families. Over the years, I have learned to be sensitive to the Holy Spirit and follow His prompting when He wants me to pray for a particular family member.

While in my extended family member's *waiting room*, I like to meditate on and profess the scripture in Psalm 37:23, "The steps of a good man are ordered by the LORD: and he delighteth in his way." I am professing that my extended family members are good, righteous, and their steps are directed by God. Therefore, God delights in their ways. This scripture helps to alleviate being stressed out and worrying about my extended family members.

Depending on the individual and their circumstances, you may be in their spiritual waiting room on a full-time or part-time basis. You may be saying, "Felicia, you make this sound like a job." Well, I say it's more like a career! Since I have taken on the mindset that it is my duty to pray and intercede for my extended family members, I have made a career of it.

A career should be a position in life that we are committed to, intentionally seeking and pursuing it with excellence. That's my attitude when it comes to my placement in the spiritual waiting room of my extended family members. I am committed to praying and interceding for them. I intentionally seek God on how to pray for my extended family members, and with a heart of excellence, I pursue peaceful ways to inquire about their specific prayer requests.

We must be approachable, remain nonjudgmental, and have empathy whenever necessary. Having a quality relationship with family members extending beyond the fact that we are related is imperative. Our kinship must also have roots grounded in a loving friendship with mutual respect for one another. This type of relationship will help foster love as it promotes the ability to be transparent. It also encourages us to ask for and accept help when the storms of life attempts to engulf us.

Just like with anyone else, when an extended family member comes to us desiring prayer, we must not use this time as an opportunity to find fault with them. But instead, use this as an opportunity to build them up, encourage, inspire, and help restore hope back into their hearts.

I am reminded of a recent phone conversation that I had with my Auntie Joyce who lives in another state. The nature of my phone call was to check on my aunt and get a second opinion regarding some hair products that my daughter was trying to educate me on. My aunt is a licensed professional hairstylist. She's an excellent resource for advice regarding my hair or anything else that I need an additional opinion on. Now, I could have contacted my local hair stylist, but I kept getting this nudging in my spirit to call my aunt. So I made the call. Actually, when she answered the phone, I thought she was my cousin, but that wasn't the case. It was my aunt on the other end of that call. It was her voice that I was hearing, but not in the jovial tone that I had grown accustomed to.

My aunt was dealing with feelings of heavy sadness. As I listened to her, I did not dismiss the emotions she was experiencing. I was no stranger to those emotions. I had to confront and tackle them myself. It wasn't just me and my aunt being disturbed by these negative feelings; the world was experiencing the same frustration. There was a great majority of us struggling with having to accept our new normal as we navigated our way through a horrific worldwide health pandemic.

Like I said, I didn't dismiss her feeling, but instead I shifted her focus to how much God loves her and that He sent His Son, Jesus Christ, to redeem her from the heaviness of sadness. She already knew this but just needed a friendly reminder. Toward the end of our conversation, those emotions of heavy sadness turned into emotions of thankfulness and gratefulness. My aunt was glad that I had called her. I was glad and thankful that I made the call. The nudging that I was experiencing was indeed the Holy Spirit prompting me to call my Auntie Joyce so that I could encourage her and help uplift her spirit.

Chapter 5

Friends

In many instances, the relationships that we have with our friends can resemble the closeness of blood-relative relationships. These are the "we are doing life together" friendships. Once we have allowed ourselves to be transparent enough for someone to get to know us like family, a mutual friendship and respect for one another is established. When it comes to being in the spiritual waiting room of a friend I think the same mindset of being in the spiritual waiting room of extended family members applies.

Several years ago, a close friend of mine called me on the phone, and she began to share with me a conversation that she and God had regarding me. She was given very specific instructions to give to me. I wrote them down so that I wouldn't forget a single word. My friend was in the *waiting room* for me. I knew she was in there. She had been there for a few years waiting in exuberant expectation for me to receive my breakthrough. My instructions from God were, *Start cleaning out your house. Get ready! Get ready! Your breakthrough is now! Trust, believe, and receive!* I was also given this scripture to meditate on: "For I know the thoughts that I think toward you, saith the LORD, thoughts of peace, and not of evil, to give you an expected end" (Jeremiah 29:11).

For several years, I had been praying for a more accommodating house for me, my husband, and our three teenagers. I told my family that we should began praying corporately for our new home. They agreed, and we did. We had out grown the house that we were living in at that time. Mentally, I had already moved us forward; I imagined us being in our new home. I followed the instructions that God gave me. We positioned ourselves to become recipients of the breakthrough that God was preparing for us. I began cleaning out the closets and the basement. These where the major reservoirs of clutter in my house during that time.

My husband and I readied ourselves by paying off debt, saving a substantial down payment, packing items that weren't being utilized on a daily basis, and hired an excellent realtor. We also increased our offerings to our local church and to other ministries. Although this was an exciting time for us, it was also a very hectic time as well. It was difficult coordinating our schedules so that my husband and I both could be available for a house viewing. There was an issue with the mortgage company; some of our documents had been misplaced. We would place a bid on a house, get excited, only to have someone outbid us; which was an extremely frustrating process.

Being that it was a "seller's market" at that time, houses where priced high and off the market quickly. It surely was a daunting task trying to stay ahead of the other potential buyers. I think my Jessica was in competition with our relator—no, I am just kidding! Remember what I said regarding Jessica acquiring exceptional leadership capabilities. Without anyone asking her, attempting to give our family a competitive edge, Jessica diligently searched the internet in her free time in hopes of finding our new home. As it turned out, Jessica did discover the house that my family now calls *home*. We stayed in faith, stood our ground, and kept a positive attitude. Eighteen months later from the time that I received that phone call from my friend, we purchased a house that was more suitable and accommodating for our family. That house continues to be a blessing to us, and it is a constant reminder of God's faithfulness, goodness, and mercy toward us.

Chapter 6

Your Neighbors

As I refer to our neighbors in this chapter, I am not speaking of the neighbors that we turn to greet while we are at church. However, I am referring to the neighbors who are literally the people that live alongside you in your neighborhood. Being that our homes are our living quarters, it's our place of refuge from the outside world. The connection that we have with our neighbors is vitally important. Our relationship with our neighbors will definitely have an impact on the quality of our lives while we are neighbors.

Many neighbors develop friendships that evolve over a lifetime and still remain intact when either of them moves away from the neighborhood. This is the case for my family and the neighbor that lived next door to us in our previous neighborhood. My family still keeps in contact with this neighbor. We moved next door to her when our eldest daughter was a toddler, our youngest daughter was a newborn, and our son wasn't even born yet.

We did life with this neighbor. She became our friend, confidante, babysitter, and she is a fellow church member. She made home ownership a pleasant experience for us being that this was our first house that we had purchased, and we had just started raising our young family. Well, we didn't know it at the time, but we later found out that she had been praying for us all along.

Shortly after we had moved in and began building a friendship with our new neighbor, she informed us of her prayers for a family with young children to buy the house next to hers. Well, that's exactly what happened; God answered her prayers. My husband and I noticed the vacant house while on a fast-food run. I was pregnant with our youngest daughter, and she had me craving Mexican food. Martin drove in pursuit of finding some satisfactory food for a craving pregnant woman, whose antennas were glazing up and down streets hunting for realtor signs planted in front lawns of potential sellers.

My neighbor was praying for my family. Praying for neighbors that she had never seen or met before. Looking back on it, my neighbor was in my family's *waiting room* praying for our future. My family became the benefactors of her prayers. Although we had not met the acquaintance of this beautiful, kindhearted lady, she had already greatly impacted our lives for the better. As my young family continued to grow with the birth of our son and many other milestone events, she has been there right beside us praying with and for us. Her love and commitment to the well-being of my family continues, although my family has move to another city. The Wright family is truly grateful to have her in our lives. I pray that one day my family can pay it forward and be the kind of neighbor that she has been to us.

Chapter 7

The Workplace

Individuals in the workplace are people who are usually in our lives because we work together. Hence, we have a working relationship. If you are not working for or with a relative, this relationship was forged because you in some form or another work for the same company. As a result, this relationship materialized. My point is that this relationship would not exist if we were not coworkers. However, we should not minimize our role in this relationship just because we are coworkers. As you might have already experienced, we have the ability to impact the lives of others in the workplace. We should be forever mindful that God has given us our place of employment as a platform not only to financially benefit us but to also be an instrumental force assisting Him in reaching others. And as we do His will, He will transform us into a constant, beautiful, open display of His love and power.

I believe our coworkers and employers should know that we are Christians. As Christians, we must understand the importance of letting our light shine wherever we are, and this includes the workplace. But we are to do this for His glory and not our own. We must remember that our employers are not paying us to witness Jesus Christ to our coworkers. Our performance should be the letting our "light shine" and the witness of our relationship that we have with Jesus Christ.

When we operate in the highest level of integrity and become an exemplary employee, we are letting our light shine. God is pleased because we are representing Him well. We become valuable assets to our employers, and then God will allow us to be used as "a person of influence" in the lives of our coworkers and employer. Remember we must stay humble, walk in love and integrity at all times. Make no mistake about it, this platform will at times come with much persecution and criticism. However, our Lord and Savior will always protect you and be the lifter of your head when you do things His way.

We should train our children to operate in this manner at their workplace as well. I am reminded of the time when one of my daughters told me she believed that God was leading her to pray for her coworker and the coworker's family. She asked me to pray for them during my personal prayer time. It is not unusual for my children to ask me to agree with them in prayer regarding coworkers and work-related issues.

This occasion was different. She enlisted help from her dad and I, we went to her actual workplace to pray. We came into agreement with our daughter when we joined our faith with hers as she prayed for her fellow coworker and her family. I was moved to tears at the act of compassion my daughter had for her coworker and the boldness she operated in to carry out what she believed in her heart God had instructed her to do.

Let me also say this, my daughter was given consent from her coworker for us to pray with them. It is prudent to get permission from the coworker prior to praying with them. You do not want your coworker to feel like they were coerced or ambushed into praying. However, you definitely want to follow the leading of the Holy Spirit before you physically pray with them. Follow His leading, and He will do the rest.

Having a good work relationship with other Christians is also influential and beneficial to our spiritual growth. The scripture that comes to mind is in Proverbs 27:17, "Iron sharpeneth iron; so a man sharpeneth the countenance of his friend." This relationship will help keep us sharp in addition to being a support system for each other. Several years ago, I worked for an agency as a part-time employee. The company was facing some financial challenges as they were phasing out my position and incorporating a limited number of full-time positions. I didn't have the required seniority to qualify for any of the full-time positions. However, another Christian whom I had a good work relationship with, unbeknownst to me, was praying that I would get one of the full-time positions.

God gave me favor, and I was granted one of the full-time positions. I later found out that this coworker was asked to be on the committee that selected the full-time recipients. I didn't know it at the time, but during that entire process, she was rooting for me and claimed one of the full-time positions for me.

I would also encourage you to pray for your entire management team and employer. In 1 Timothy 2:1–3, it reads:

> I exhort therefore, that, first of all, supplication, prayers, intercessions, and giving of thanks, be made for all men; For kings, and for all that are in authority; that we may lead a quiet and peaceable life in all godliness and honesty. For this is good and acceptable in the sight of God our Saviour.

Usually the individuals that come to mind with these Bible verses are the president of the United States, other government officials, and anyone else in a position of authority. This scripture is also befitting for the workplace. To a degree, our supervisors, managers, and employers all have some form of authority over us.

We all need peace at our place of employment. Many of us spend more awaking hours at work than we do at our personal homes, thus making our place of employment our second home. A peaceful work environment helps contribute to our overall spiritual well-being, which ultimately affects our physical and mental state. Anxiety in the workplace affects productivity and employee morale. As we watch the news on TV and engage in everyday life activities, we are exposed to employees who are becoming more and more disgruntled. They are taking matters in their own hands and bringing harm to themselves and their coworkers. We definitely need the peace of God in our workplaces.

So let's make sure that we are operating in the peace of God while we are in the workplace. Having His peace will help us stay alert, vigilant, and sensitive to the Holy Spirit. This will allow us to move in the direction that He leads and guides us during our time spent in our coworkers' *waiting room*.

Chapter 8

Yourself

The question is, how do you deal with yourself while you are in your very own spiritual waiting room? Well, for starters, you must identify that you are in your own *waiting room*. We have become accustomed to taking care of and praying for others that we oftentimes put our prayers for ourselves on the back burner. While our waiting room issues are on a slow boil to simmer, we must implement the same level of fervency and expectation to ourselves. We must stand our ground and not back down nor give in to the temptation of getting weary and giving up.

Let me use myself as an example. Over the years, I have had countless waiting room experiences that have required me to remain patient, consistent in prayer, and hopeful. Keeping my faith has not always been easy, but I knew that it was necessary in order for me to obtain the manifestation of my prayers. There are several scriptures that I pray, profess, and meditate on when I am in my own waiting room. Here are a few of them:

> Trust in the LORD with all thine heart; and lean not unto thine own understanding. In all thy ways acknowledge him, and he shall direct thy paths. (Proverbs 3:5–6)

> Be careful for nothing; but in every thing by prayer and supplication with thanksgiving let your requests be made known unto God. (Philippians 4:6)

Let us take a look at my own waiting room experience with writing this book. This book was several years in the making before I finally penned my final thoughts on *The Waiting Room*. In its infancy, I would write a few paragraphs then stop. When a thought came to mind, I would write it down on whatever type of paper that was available. Scrap sheets of paper, the back of envelopes, whatever form of paper that was at my disposal I utilized to convey and record my thoughts. Might I add, this was pre-smartphone era. With today's technology, I can just record what I am thinking on my smartphone.

No one knew I was writing a book. It wasn't until I showed my oldest daughter Jessica part of the introduction that I began to hold myself accountable and push past my writer's block. Jessica had to write a short story for her English class, and she was experiencing some writer's block of her own. I explained to her that was normal and encouraged her to keep trying. I expressed to her I was having the same issue. She looked bewildered (as I previously stated, no one knew I was working on a writing project). I showed her my last written entry. To her surprise, she saw and read physical proof that I was truly writing a book. She said to me, "Mom, you wrote this? I didn't know that you could write!" Seeing the amazement on her face was really encouraging to me. I didn't realize it at the time, but I had just outed myself and signed on an accountability partner.

Somehow my other daughter Ashley discovered that I was writing a book. Then she became a self-appointed accountability partner. They would ask me, "Mom, when was the last time you did any writing?" This was their way of saying, *We are rooting for you. We are counting on you to finish what you have started. Don't give up, Mom, you can do this!* My daughters were cheering me on, they had become my cheerleaders. Their excitement for me to become a published author has truly been inspirational.

I later told my husband, my parents, my spiritual big sister, a few coworkers, an aunt, and an uncle of my desire to get serious about writing. They all were very supportive and encouraging. Last year, some of my colleagues rallied in support of me, they were ecstatic to find out about this hidden talent of mine. Now I have my very own village of support.

My Uncle Andrew would occasionally check in on me and lovingly urge me to continue pursuing my dream of becoming a published author. This same uncle is a writer and published author himself. He recently said something that resonated within me. He simply stated that his book "will be a witness for him when he is no longer here." I have always considered an author's book to be an extension of their legacy. But after pondering upon my uncle's viewpoint, the word *witness* struck a chord with me.

The way I perceived him saying the word *witness* was in the form of a noun and a verb. *Witness* in the form of a noun is his actual physical book, the tangible evidence that he wrote his book. Then there is *witness* in the form of a verb, which is providing action. *Witness* is now written words turning into communicative dialogue. My uncle's voice is now speaking to others conveying information, knowledge, experience, and most importantly testifying. That one word *witness*, and how I perceived it as a noun and a verb has compelled me to finally finish composing what I started several years ago. Inspired by my uncle's words, I also want my writings to be a witness now and in the future.

Whether your own waiting room experience is regarding your health, finances, career, relationships, or turning a hobby into a lucrative business venture; you can experience peace and victory while you are in your own *Waiting Room*.

About the Author

Felicia M. Wright is a native of Detroit, Michigan. She is a registered nurse who presently works in private duty home healthcare. Her bachelor's degree in nursing was obtained from Oakland University, Rochester, Michigan. She currently resides in West Bloomfield, Michigan, with her husband Martin, and they have three adult children. Felicia has been passionate about writing since her childhood. She is a food connoisseur, enjoys hosting family gatherings, and taking long scenic walks with her husband.

CPSIA information can be obtained
at www.ICGtesting.com
Printed in the USA
BVHW080203090721
611407BV00002B/67